# Boss Chronicles

## Jackie Johnson

Copyright ©2018 Jackie Johnson

"Boss Chronicles"

Publisher: Manifested Truth Publishing

Printed in the United States of America

ISBN: 978-1719025034

All rights reserved solely by the author. The author guarantees all contents are original and do not infringe upon the legal rights of any other person or work. No part of this book may be reproduced in any form without the permission of the author.

Unless otherwise indicated, all Scripture quotations are taken from the King James Version of the Holy Bible.

Unless otherwise noted, all word definitions are taken from the Merriam-Webster online dictionary.

# DEDICATION

This book is dedicated to my mother, Ms. Dorthy Bryant. Through all of the bad, God still used you to show me how to be strong, resilient, loving, and GREAT! I pray, that you are not only proud of me but also, the legacy my children are walking in; knowing that it all began with you. **All things** do work together for **the good** of them who **Love God** and are Called according to **HIS PURPOSE**.

To my three amazing Teenpreneurs & Superstars; Mikel, Mi'Kayla, and Mikah; you inspire me every day. Thank you for being such an amazing reflection and representation of me and all I taught & showed you. I am beyond proud of your intelligence, resilience, heart, and achievements. Live fearlessly in the now but NEVER FORGET that the future belongs to you IF you continue to keep God first.

# CONTENTS

**DEDICATION** ..............................................

**CH. 1** *"Scheduling is Crucial"* ........................... 1

**CH. 2** *"Work Environment"* ............................. 6

**CH. 3** *"Paint a Picture"* ................................ 14

**CH. 4** *"Educate Yourself"* .............................. 19

**CH. 5** *"Integrity is a Must"* ............................ 24

**CH. 6** *"Self-Maintenance"* .............................. 35

**CH. 7** *"Supporting is Networking"* ..................... 42

**CH. 8** *"Separate the Finances"* ......................... 50

**CH. 9** *"Boss-Like Behavior"* ............................ 57

**CH. 10** *"Boss Up"* ..................................... 66

**ABOUT THE AUTHOR** ................................... 78

# 1
## *Scheduling is Crucial*

There are a lot of truly talented and determined entrepreneurs in the world today; but not all of them understand that it takes more than talent, ability, and resilience to be a "Boss". One of the major things that can stunt the growth and success of any entrepreneur is the inability to utilize proper time management skills.

You can have the best service and/or product in the world, but if you lack the knowledge of time management or the discipline needed to follow the plan/schedule you create, then you will be halted in the middle of your success. You don't want to cap the potential of your business before you've even had the chance to explore what you and your business is truly capable of.

Time management requires you to take a detailed look at everything you need and want to do. You then must prioritize those lists in order of importance and necessity. Once you've done this; now you can map out a plan or create a schedule to ensure that the tasks are accomplished.

A lot of people hate going through all of the extra steps (they think) to do this, but I can promise you one thing: the moment you learn and apply scheduling to your life, things will run a whole lot smoother.

You cannot be a "Boss" by winging every day of your life. This may work for some individuals briefly; but the moment your business starts growing and expanding, something is going to fall through the cracks, because none of us are human computer systems. Running a business is full of information, details, procedures, etc. that we are just not equipped to handle without developing a business module "personal system of handling your business' operating functions".

I want to be very clear in saying that using proper time management skills is not just a business benefit, but it's a life benefit as well. It's beneficial for your home life just as well as your business life. The truth is that entrepreneurs usually start off working from their homes. As you grow as a business you may isolate your business to a specific area of the home, but you'll still be home based. This is another reason why a daily schedule will be extremely beneficial to the entrepreneur especially.

If you're anything like me, then you can relate to the fact that I wanted to make money, be my own boss, and not ever have to leave my bed on the hard or sick days. I desired to do all of those things, but I also didn't want to be too exhausted to help my kids with their homework or hear about their day at school. I didn't want to fall asleep on my husband when he wanted to share with me the highs and lows of his day, and I definitely didn't want to be too exhausted when it was time for husband and wife intimacy time.

The sad reality is that many entrepreneurs are too tired, do miss their children's events and special moments; all in the name of "the grind". Some people will tell you that you have to be willing to sacrifice everything including some family time to become more successful quicker; this is simply because many people put more value on working harder. However, I am not one of them. I believe in the "working smarter, not harder" method.

When I take the time to schedule my day out, I can maximize my time more efficiently. I noticed that I didn't waste as much time, and I didn't feel so drained or bored (which both are common side effects of new entrepreneurship). I have a great, productive, and happy day when I create and follow my schedule. Your winning must be intentional; not just because God said you would be successful, but because your continued efforts show proof that you believed God when he said it.

# 2
## Work Environment

Within the early/beginning stages of entrepreneurship many people struggle with maintaining a balance between home and business. This is so ironic because, most women entrepreneurs are motivated to be their own boss, so they can be home for their families in the first place, without the finances of the home suffering because of their decision. Some people believe that women have become too independent and too focused on being self-sufficient. It's assumed that these qualities have taken away their desire to be homemakers anymore. I don't believe that to be the case; at least it isn't for me because I enjoy being a mother and an attentive wife to my husband. It brings me a peace and joy that allows me to run my businesses with confidence, passion, and great joy.

The economics of today no longer make it realistic to take care of a family and household with just one income, especially if the income is under the National average household salary of $53,000 a year. Keep in mind that although this is the national average, many households bring in much less.

According to the Census Bureau, a family of four needs $49,114 a year just to cover rent, utilities, food, transportation, necessities, and childcare. For the households that do earn the average salary of $53,000; there's only $3,886 a year left to save, enjoy entertainment, take a vacation, handle vehicle maintenance, and everything else they need and want for their families. Now imagine the families that don't even bring in $30,000 a year. This is where the poverty and day to day struggles come in at.

This is the source of extra stress and worries upon the shoulders of families and the individual or individuals that are financially responsible to take care of the family unit. These struggles are the main reasons why the single mother or father are working multiple jobs and may not get to spend much time with their children.

The single parent has no time for dating and other needed social outings/engagements that are essential outlets for adults to have healthy social skills. The single parent has no time for any of this because they're working all the time, and when they get a moment free, they have to take care of the house, the kids, or just rest because they never get any.

When you make the decision to take the leap of faith into entrepreneurship, it's not a luxury at first. When you first start your business, it's a necessity. You must succeed, because if you don't then your household goes into lack and despair. The bills are depending on you and the kids are depending on you too. Think about your reasons for taking the leap. Use whatever motivation you have to start your business and be dedicated to making it successful and keep that in the forefront of your mind. Let it fuel you to pursue it with all diligence.

Therefore, after you've gotten your plan ready, and you've created your daily schedule as an entrepreneur; it's now time to go into "Beast Mode"! Beast Mode is how we describe that gut feeling, that eagle eye focus, and the brave heart of a lion. In order to execute your vision and plan to become successful you have to be resilient and tough. Be determined from day one not to allow fear, disappointment, or intimidation to hinder your efforts.

In this chapter, I want to deal with your "work environment". Just because you're working from home, doesn't mean that you get to lay around in the bed all day and work when you feel like it. It's now time to take that same energy, work ethic, punctuation, and professionalism that you gave to that nine to five job you came off of; and apply it to your own business.

You will need to create a workspace within your home. The type of business you have will help to determine the amount and type of space you need. You may just need an office. Some people will need a worktable to create or build.

Outline what kind of workspace you need and make it your own. You have a great opportunity to make your work environment fun, bright, motivating, etc. This is another way to encourage yourself consistently. For example, I do most of my work from the computer. I do ship things, so I need a small space to store items until they're ready to be sent to the customer or until they're needed to display at a vendor show. My set up of a small office in my bedroom works perfectly for me. I have some privacy within my bedroom and enough room to carve out a workspace. At one point in the beginning stages of my family's online boutique; I turned my living room (because we rarely entertained guest within our home) into my online boutique's showroom. This worked well for my household; you will have to discover what works well for yours.

The reason why your workspace is necessary, is because it helps to create your work environment. Almost everyone I know that still works a nine to five job, complains about the environment of their jobs, from not having pleasant bosses, to meddling co-workers, to strict time constraints, etc. Now that you're working from home; your work environment will be whatever you choose it to be. Sometimes, I like to listen to music because it triggers my creative juices. I couldn't just turn on my music at a nine to five because I would have to be considerate of all the other employees around me.

Your work environment should be one that inspires productivity and success. My sons helped me to paint the walls in my corner office pink. We added gold foil circles, and I kept the desk and chair I first started with in my business because it held sentimental value for me. I have a photo of my dream home on the wall framed. It's positioned on the wall directly in front of my desk so that I can be inspired and reminded why I do what I'm doing.

I have all the things I love in my office such as candles, flowers, inspirational quotes, and a whole lot of bling. When you walk into the room, you know it belongs to me. I even have a single cup Keurig machine on my desk because I love coffee and tea. When I step into my workspace every day, I'm charged and inspired to make magic. Get visual with planning/creating your perfect workspace so that you can create a positive, light, empowering work environment that you'll be excited to go work in each day.

# 3
## Paint a Picture

As an entrepreneur, be aware that building your brand and the brand of your business is the absolute same thing. Until your business reaches a place of notoriety and it completely speaks for itself, your appearance is EVERYTHING! When you're on social media, in church, at sporting events, school functions, even the grocery store, you need to look like "success". I'm not telling you to spend money that you don't have on name brand things, (we'll discuss this later) because that is a serious no-no while you are brand building.

Everything about you should be painting a beautiful masterpiece to the public (who are potentially your future clients and/or customers). Your clothing should reflect you and your uniqueness. Your wardrobe should be clean, neat, and somehow noticeable. If your style is similar to someone else that's already gained notoriety/status, add something small but special that can later be associated with you.

This doesn't mean that you have to walk around looking like a schoolteacher or an accountant unless that is your business. You want to carry a look of professionalism while adding a chunk of individualism. For instance, I may dress business casual when meeting my writing and publishing clients, but I spice it up with my hair color or some Afro centric earrings or hoops, maybe even a headwrap. Think about the image you want to show people, create it, and then be aware of it every time you leave the house.

Painting a picture isn't just about your outward presentation. It's also about the attitude and vibes that you give off to others, especially when people are meeting you for the first time. This can be a difficult task for those of you who can be a little introverted at times. Introverts hate social gatherings. They are not fond of networking and/or speaking to strangers in general. They definitely hate large crowds. However, to my introvert entrepreneurs, I must challenge you to search for ways to seem more social, even if it gives your stomach the biggest case of butterflies ever. You don't have to be the life of the party, but you have to make sure that your tone and body's disposition when interacting with others doesn't convey a lackadaisical or irritated presence.

You also want to be careful that you don't seem arrogant or dismissive to individuals as well. These two things are absolute turn offs for potential customers and clients. Think about it, would you want to spend your hard-earned money with someone you felt like thought they were better than you? Most people would rather spend their money with the business owner that was confident yet friendly.

I'm only cautioning you about this topic because, the pride you feel as a person that was bold enough to do what most people want to do, but are just too afraid or uneasy to do, can be mis-interpreted and mis-represented. Just remember to be professional and courteous but also try to allow the greatest parts of who you are draw people in. Let your disposition and great customer service make them want to know where your success comes from. Be everything you want the businesses you patronize to be.

# 4
## Educate Yourself

Whatever products or services your business provides, make sure that you're great at it or that you have a passion for it. This is the key to having a successful, ever growing engine of success. We as human beings tend to do well in the things we love to do. People go to college for years, obtain degree after degree, and even work years on jobs before they end up quitting to start a business doing the hobby they've had since high school, or the side jobs they created to earn extra money for their household.

When you devise a plan to make money doing what you love; it feels like all the answers to the world's mysteries become apparent to you. Many of us run towards success with immeasurable zeal but may still be lacking the knowledge and wisdom needed to be a total package. This is the reason why you must continue to educate yourself as an entrepreneur. Often times we focus on our strengths but totally ignore our weaknesses.

As an entrepreneur, your business will have obvious strengths. Identifying them will be the easy part for most. The hard part is identifying the things that can cause your business to fail, or cause clients/customers to not want to do business with you. When you identify these things; you're now ready to start educating yourself on the subject.

We exist in a time and age where the internet can be a great asset for you. The internet puts most knowledge at your very fingertips so, there is never an excuse to lack or not get better in your business practices. There are many free resources to learn about any and everything you may need to know in order to run a successful business. Never be ashamed to seek out help or information if you're not able to grasp the information on your own. Some information will come easy for a self-learner, but other things you may decide that you don't want to go through that much trouble. I want to encourage you here and let you know that there is nothing wrong with feeling this way. Remember to always work smarter not harder. If it makes sense to hire someone to do the job, then hire someone.

One of the worst things you can do as entrepreneur, is trying to do everything by yourself. You need to cut yourself some slack in the areas that you feel less than adequate in affectively performing. When you go to a restaurant, imagine what the experience would be like, if the owner greeted you as the hostess, took your order as the waiter, and then went into the kitchen to cook your meal, and then came back to serve it to you with a smile. That would be nice if you bought out the place and you and your company were the only guests, but it would be a disaster if there were multiple customers waiting to be served as well.

Sometimes, small business owners think they can handle everything because they're small or because they're used to doing everything themselves. They may not have anyone else to train or rely on that's willing to help for free until finances start flowing regularly. However, this thought pattern is counterproductive.

Your clientele or customer base may be small now, but the idea is to be able to master small business so that you can grow effortlessly with your client/customer base. You cannot wait until you become a big business to be ready. You have to prepare and run your business from day one as if it's already a successful business that's servicing a large amount of people and taking in a large amount of revenue.

I have a quote that I say to myself and to my business mentees, "*If you see yourself where you're going then you won't be stuck where you are.*" People who wait to put policies in place are often times overwhelmed or sabotaged by the unexpected influx of business.

# 5
## *Integrity is a Must*

Have you ever done business with an entrepreneur before, but it went horribly to the left? I have too unfortunately, and that's the reason why this chapter is so important. It's difficult when you're preaching and telling everyone around you to buy local, shop with entrepreneurs, and spend money within your own communities but when you do, you're met with unprofessionalism and bad character.

The Webster's dictionary defines integrity as, a firm adherence to a code of especially moral or artistic values. This simply implies that integrity is when you have a strong belief in your personal morals or life code. It may seem irrelevant to business practices, but that's not true, especially for entrepreneurs.

Entrepreneurs/Small Businesses are judged more harshly than big corporations. It may not be fair, but consumers want to understand what the benefit of buying from the small businesses truly is, as opposed to the big-name stores and companies they've been purchasing goods and services from for most of their lives.

Having impeccable integrity is where the small business can stand out. Take my family's online boutique for example, although most of our items are lower than our local and corporate competitors, we still have many obstacles we encounter. We pay higher costs because we don't order in large enough quantities which makes us have to charge a little more than we'd like to sometimes to make a profit.

It also used to take an extremely long time for shipping because our items were coming directly from Chinese manufacturers. We would be forced to pay higher shipping rates for "expedited shipping" which wasn't really expedited at all because they took a 4-day processing time and then 5-7 business days for shipping, which meant our customers were waiting between 12 – 15 business days to receive their orders.

Our last and major issue we encountered was the real fit of the items, because the items were manufactured in China, we often weren't able to gage the real fit of the item because Chinese manufactured clothing is way smaller than the

American standard sizing and their charts were not always accurate.

The interesting thing about our list of obstacles is, that they are common obstacles for stores and boutiques alike. Every business must assess its strengths and weaknesses to become a better competitor and a stronger, steadier establishment.

A business' uniqueness as well as its obstacles must be evaluated in order to properly be prepared to handle the issues with professionalism, great customer service, and impeccable integrity. The other thing I want you to understand and know is, that no business (weather corporate or local) is perfect. Every business makes mistakes and/or runs into problems. However, knowing how to properly handle the moments when things don't go right will be a deciding factor in determining if a customer will do repeat business with you.

My family's businesses can safely estimate that our customer service and integrity has accounted for about 85% of our repeat customers and clients. That number makes me extremely proud and happy. As a business owner, you must also be able to stand out by caring about the people you serve. Your product and/or services are not exclusive to just you. Let's face it; there are people out there who can do exactly what you do, and some may even be a little better at it. What you must ask yourself is, "can they do it like I do it?" Do you make your customers/clients feel valued and appreciated? Do you make them feel like their order, project, or inquiry is of the utmost importance to you? When your company makes a mistake or inconveniences someone, do you have set things in place to apologize and compensate them for it?

The details of some of the most horrible experiences I have personally had doing business locally have been bad attitudes and them refusing to issue refunds for services not rendered or improperly completed.

I'll be completely transparent and honest by saying, that sometimes it cost you money to operate with integrity, but it also teaches you to not make the same mistakes twice. Other times it will cause you to re-evaluate your process to make your business practices more effective.

Once you have identified obstacles for your business, you now have to come up with solutions to minimize or eliminate its occurrence. Remember earlier in this chapter, I identified my business' obstacles of paying higher cost on items (because we don't buy in bulk), the shipping time, and the real fit and quality of the items being unknown. We had to come up with solutions for our business to be able to minimize the issues we were having stemming from those three issues.

For our first issue of paying higher cost for items; we decided not to purchase items above a certain dollar amount so that we could keep our prices under $50. This allowed us to sell quality items for reasonable prices, while still allowing us to make a decent profit. We also kept track of our frequently ordered items to obtain stock that will be appealing for our pop-up shops and vendor events.

The second issue of "long shipping times", was really not within our control as far as making the items get to us quicker. We became very transparent and honest with our customers about the shipping time by posting the delivery time frames in each item's description area, so that no one would be shocked after paying for an item. This allowed our customers to make the decision if they wanted to wait the two weeks for delivery or not. We found out that if you're honest with people, give them the necessary information, and give them the freedom to decide; they were very appreciative and supportive. If they were in a rush or needed the item for something specific, they may not get that item but they would come back and shop because they couldn't believe that we didn't trick them like other places, by not advising of the delivery time until after they had already paid.

When it comes to integrity, "honesty really is the best policy". My third issue of not knowing the true fit and quality of the item was a rough one. The truth is, quality is going to vary for each client based on their taste and preference. Half of this battle was won by including the material the item was made with in the description. It was more time consuming on our part when putting it on the website, but it was a time-consuming job that made our lives a little easier on the back end.

The other half of that battle was won by taking the time to find and convert the listed Chinese measurements by comparing them to the U.S. standard measurement chart. So, when we placed the item on the website, we wrote down the U.S sizes instead of what was listed. Later we found manufactures in the U.S. which cut our delivery times in half.

Before we worked out the kinks, we had customers that didn't like the quality of an item; our policy was no refunds, but we did allow exchanges. In other instances when the size was completely off, and we didn't have a size that would fit the customer or if it was going to cause our customer to have to wait another long wait time; we refunded them. This is what

I meant when I said, "sometimes it will cost you money to operate with integrity". In those cases, we lost money because the company's either didn't give refunds or by the time you did everything, they asked to get a refund back, it was so long to wait, but you had to give the money form your business' account right away. In these cases, we took a loss that put us in the red or caused me to have to cover from my personal money, but I would rather have a low account in an effort to maintain the pride in my business' actions and giving my best effort not to hurt or inconvenience my customer just to make a couple of dollars.

I want you to remember that it will be hard sometimes to do the right thing, but you will be happy that your business flourished while treating people with a pleasant attitude and demeanor, as well as being fair with them.

Always write down your business' polices and advise customers and clients before accepting payments. You do this to cover you and your business' liability with each customer/client. Be upfront with people about what you provide and what you expect in return. If you make those things clear from the beginning, then it's hard to encounter misunderstandings that lead to dissatisfaction.

# 6
## Self-Maintenance

If you're anything like me; you want everyone that you love to make it to the top with you. You are always thinking of others and you're extremely conscious about how you can help make their lives better. This is of course, an awesome way to be. Love, compassion, and sacrifice are honorable traits to have, especially when dealing with others. However, I'm just going to be honest with you right here in this moment and tell you, "everyone you love and support will not show you the same love and support back." Most people know this in their mind but still have difficulty processing it in their heart.

You must realize that everyone is not you. Everyone doesn't think the way you do, nor will they show their love in action the way you are willing to. Being an entrepreneur will be emotionally difficult at times because of these very reasons. No matter how hard it may become; you've got to continue building your business and your brand. You will have friends, family, and associates who just will not support, believe in, or promote you as an entrepreneur. In the eyes of some people, you will always just be "you". They will love you as their friend, family, sweet lady, or man but they will not look at you and see the business guru, the marketing genius, or the witty inventor. Their viewpoint and opinions cannot become stumbling blocks for you. You cannot allow their disposition towards you to create any kind of bitterness within your heart whatsoever.

You may be asking yourself, "what does any of this have to do with being an entrepreneur". I'm happy to explain why your emotional placement is directly tied to entrepreneurship. Entrepreneurs must be bold, confident, and resilient. Building a business many times from nothing or limited resources is a miracle all in itself. It's helpful when you have a great support team but that will often not be your case. So, you will need to be self-motivated to do the impossible. You will experience setbacks, mistakes, and disasters in attempting to create a great working flow and establishing your business' special niche.

You cannot create greatness if you don't believe in yourself and your ability to make your business successful. When people that are closest to us seem to lack support for us, it can vastly affect our self-perception as well as bring doubt into the picture. Therefore, self-maintenance is crucial for you if you're going to emerge as an entrepreneurial force to be reckoned with.

There are several components to self-maintenance. The first component is being connected to healthy, functional, and positive people. The last thing you want to do, is keep a "Negative Nancy" around you when you're trying to do something that most people don't have the courage to do. Some people will pretend to be excited about your decision, but every word that comes out of their mouth will contradict their statement of support.

The second component to self-maintenance is to learn to put yourself first for a change. Most of us are trying to build for the sake of others, most often our family. Other times, we're building to just be in a better position to help others to be able to do better in life. However, we often forget to take care of ourselves. We forget to enjoy the fruits of our own labor. Build for the sake of saving, to take a vacation some place you've always dreamed of visiting, or take a class/attend a workshop to better educate yourself in your business' field, etc. But think of yourself as well as building to help others.

The third and final component of self-maintenance is your energy source. Your energy source is where you draw strength, motivation, and joy from. This can vary depending on the person. My personal energy source is my relationship with God. God has proven himself to be the one "CONSTANT & CONSISTENT" person and thing in my life. I

KNOW that God has always ordained and desired nothing but Greatness for me. I draw my personal strength, motivation, and joy from our interactions.

My second energy source would be my immediate family (husband and kids). We're fun, goofy, loving, and supportive of one another; especially my kids. They keep me joyful and youthful with our interactions. Stress, worry, fear, and doubt are all draining emotions and so it's important to fill your life with encounters and experiences that produce the opposite emotional responses from you.

Whatever sprit/disposition you operate in on a day to day basis; will be the very disposition/spirit that you'll translate into your business or services. The bottom line is that your happiness is your responsibility alone. You cannot control the actions of others, but you will always be able to control your reaction to them, so always choose to be the "Boss You". Don't focus on your haters, just embrace your supporters, and be your biggest fan and cheerleader.

# 7
## Supporting is Networking

A pet peeve of mine as an entrepreneur and a person in general, is when people want you to support them financially, but they won't support anyone else in the same fashion. That absolutely causes my eyes to roll to the back of my head. This seems to be a difficult lesson for some business owners to learn, grasp, and practice. Entrepreneurship is more about creating value for the dollars spent within your communities and neighborhoods.

If you support local businesses before you support big corporations then you directly impact the economic wealth where you live. I know that this point is not always as obvious as most of us think it is. There was a time not too long ago that I didn't understand this principle either. I have always been a supporter of others because it's just the way I'm built. It makes me feel a sense of pride to see other people prospering by their creative ability and the hard work of their hands.

I feel this way regardless of their color or ethnicity, but if I'm honest I'm especially excited to see a Black American, a Hispanic, a woman, or a kingdom believer doing it. However, the more I learned about economics (in effort to change my own economic demographics) the more I understood how to maximize my dollar.

When you become a business owner; you become part of that community business that can add or take away value from a neighborhood or community. Most business owners are one-tracked in their mindset. The only thing they focus on or are concerned with is, "making money". Now, hear me when I say, "it is in no wise wrong to desire to make money", but if all you care about is making money, then you're not going to be a good entrepreneur.

It takes more than a great product or service, more than a great personality, more than business savvy, or more than great marketing to make a successful business operate properly. It also takes love of one's community and attention to the people, businesses, and social consciousness of those that surround you. Being an entrepreneur allows you to directly impact those around you. Your business provides a small part of what our society as a whole is in desperate need of or has a desire to receive as a consumer.

You have to do more than have a great business to shift the economic mind and physical state of your community. We instead need to create a network of support. This network should include at least one business that provides every service we humanly need or could want as consumers. If your business is a grocery store, your neighbor's business is a landscaping company, and my business is a transportation service; then we now have a network of at least three community-based businesses that we can as a neighborhood and community support/patronize.

If you look at this selfishly, you will see the need to compete with other small businesses for revenue. However, if you view this information on a larger scale, then you understand just how important it is to shop with one another as business owners. Many other ethnic groups, set great examples of building businesses because they will all live together, work, earn money, and give the same amount into a pot to resurrect one business at a time and establish one family at a time.

As a business owner, you cannot talk to people and expect their mindsets to change overnight. You must continue to encourage and challenge them by explaining the importance of buying local, how it affects them and their families, and what that could possibly change for the future. Above everything else, you've got to mirror that lifestyle of love, giving, supporting, and community by example as well as words. All I'm really saying is that it's time to stop asking people to support your business if you don't support others.

I hear business owners all the time talk about how irritated they become when another business owner that never shops with their business is always messaging or tagging them on social media platforms to request their support and patronage, but they've never even tried to inquire or patronize them. This causes me to earnestly encourage all other business owners not to be afraid or too stingy/selfish to extend the olive branch (offer of friendship) by supporting another business.

Now, I understand that this concept goes both ways, if you show support for someone's business but they don't support you or anyone else's business then you might want to stop spending your money with them, and I'll tell you why. Firstly, if someone is not supporting your business because they don't need your service or product that is totally different from them boycotting you in a sense. Be realistic about what you offer to the public by identifying who your customer is. What demographic needs or desires your services/products? Once you figure that out, begin to analyze what benefits your business has to offer that demographic?

If you paint houses for a living, your customer is probably not going to be a college student living in the dorm, (mostly because they don't have a house or apartment to have painted and because where they're living is not designed to be permanent). Therefore, the desire to "spruce up the place" with a fresh coat of paint is probably not going to be what they want or need. However, someone who doesn't need your service or product can still support you by referring your services to others they know that will need it.

That business owner is still showing your business support. By becoming a supporter of other businesses often, you become a part of their internal network of businesses and services. When I meet people who provide the same type of services or sell the same types of products, I usually decide who I will continually support by their support of me and/or others around me. No one can receive all of the business and never give any business.

The next time you pass up the opportunity to order someone's book, shop at someone's boutique, or buy baked goods from that young entrepreneur; take a minute and think about how your purchase, no matter how small or big will impact you, your community, and the business owner. Remember that where you show support is where your networking opportunities will begin.

# 8
## Separate the Finances

It is exciting when you make your first twenty dollars from your business. The moment your first transaction hits your hands or your account, you are convinced that you can not only do this business, but that you can make money at it. It is a great and motivating feeling, but don't allow that to cloud your judgement or your pockets.

If you're just starting your business, you may have never been taught to separate your business finances from your personal finances. When you get into the practice of doing this with your business, you will then be able to truly see how good or bad your business is doing. It is important to keep business transactions separate from your personal transactions altogether. If you can learn this concept early it will save you some time, embarrassment, and stress.

Although making your own money and not having to pay other employees can feel liberating, it can also be deceptive. After a successful day of business for instance, if you count $450 in transactions, that can give you the feeling of a great day at the office. Most people immediately are ready to spend that $450 somewhere (bills, an evening out, or some type of reward). However, this is the wrong thing to do. I repeat; this is the wrong thing to do. Depending on the nature of your business. The first thing you will want to do is document what the product cost was for each sale. This will help you to determine what your profit from that product or service was.

If you sold 10 dresses at $45 each ($450), but it cost you $300 for the dresses and the shipping and packaging cost you an additional $50, then your total profit for that day is $100. Do you see how that number is a huge difference from what hit your account that day? Now you have to decide out of your profit how much needs to go back into the business and what amount you will allocate to pay yourself.

If I decide that half goes back into the business and the other half goes to me for my wages; then $50 goes back into the business' operation cost, materials, or wherever it will be needed later. Then your pay for the day should be left in the business account to continue accumulating with each sale. The goal is to pay yourself a lump sum amount once a week. Yes, I said pay yourself once a week. Although you're not working to build someone else's business anymore, you are still working to build a business.

Business owners who allow themselves to get caught up in immediate gratification from their business' funds are more likely to misuse them. By paying yourself once a week, you exhibit discipline and you're able to truly enjoy the fruits of your labor by seeing a larger amount which more clearly represents your successful efforts. This also teaches you to observe, respect, and follow your business and personal financial plan.

There may be weeks where you decide to pay yourself a little less and add more capital to your business. There also may be weeks where you have an emergency for the business, so you decide to cut your personal pay to ensure the business has enough to fall back on. These are the areas where your freedom and wisdom as an entrepreneur will be essential and beneficial.

Every business should have a financial plan, a monthly budget, as well as short and long-term financial goals. This will help you to not become complacent or dormant within the operations of your business. These three little things will remind you even when your business is doing well, that there is still more work to do.

Many people use their personal bank accounts to do business transaction with and this is also a mistake. Often times new entrepreneurs feel that until they've reached a large intake of finances that a business account is not needed. Other entrepreneurs haven't done the legal paperwork needed to open a business account, regardless of the reason; its best to keep your business legally and financially in line.

If you physically separate your business funds from your personal ones; you will teach yourself to respect your business and you will treat it as a professional entity and not your personal piggy bank. Now, let's deal with some of the legal requirements of formulating a business within your state. You will need to file an "Articles of Incorporation" with the Secretary of State where you live. This is relevant for both the nonprofit and for-profit organization. You will also need to obtain an employer I.D. number for the sake of reporting your business' financial gains and losses with the IRS.

Some banks will also require you to submit a letter on your company's letterhead, informing them of your official/legal position with the business. This is done to verify that you have the legal authority to open a bank account on behalf of that business. It doesn't matter what stage your business is in (start up, home based, or renting a facility, etc.) these steps need to be done to protect you and to help you run a financially successful business.

# 9
## Boss-Like Behavior

There is an element to entrepreneurship that a lot of people overlook and underestimate, it's called, "great customer service". Great customer service is not just corporate lingo. Every great business can be identified most by their quality customer service skills or lack thereof. Every business owner must consistently understand that you have NO business without any customers and clients.

A successful business strives to make a great impression on its clients and customers from their very first encounter. You don't often get the opportunity to correct first impressions, especially if they're negative ones so be careful with the opportunities you are given. Treat every person with respect and dignity because you need to admit to yourself before you ever start doing business that, "you need them". Without customers and clients patronizing your business, you will have no business.

The important thing to remember when an issue happens is that you and your customer both are human. To be human in nature makes you eligible for trouble and capable of error. Try to be understanding of how your client/customer may be feeling behind any inconvenience or problem with delivering your best service or product to them. If it's your company's fault, please be apologetic and empathetic towards their disappointment and possible anger. It helps if you are also willing to compensate your customer/client in some way because of the inconvenience. When you do these three things (be understanding, be apologetic, compensate) you are more likely to keep them as a continued client/customer, even though their experience was less than great.

Many business owners only care about making a dollar and so they do not concern themselves with practices of integrity. I'll be honest and reiterate what I previously said that most times you will suffer a loss or some type of financial set back in order to do the right thing for your customer/client. That part isn't going to be fun, nor is it going to feel great. You will be faced with feelings of irritation, annoyance, and discouragement, feeling like you took two steps forward only to take 5 steps backwards. I believe that it's for this reason that some entrepreneurs fail to do what's right.

However, the truth is that being a "Boss" will cost you something sometimes. I promise you it will be worth it in the end to build a business with a reputation of doing the right things by its customers and clients. When you treat your clients/customers special and fairly, you show them that you are a person of great integrity and that they can be trusted with your business.

All problems will NOT be your business' fault. Some of the issues your clients/customers encounter will be of their own fault. When an issue arises due to the negligence of your client, this is when your understanding, patience, maturity, and wisdom will need to show up; and here's why.

Most clients/customers immediately jump to the wrong conclusions and will insist that their problem is because of your company's negligence and or error. For example, if the outfit is too small, they'll say it runs small or the measurement chart wasn't accurate. In reality as you look at the customer you can clearly see that they are not the same size as the garment they ordered.

A customer can complain that the cupcakes you're selling are too small for you to be charging $5 for one and the list of complaints will go on and on. Some of your new customers and clients will simply be "complainers" but do me a favor when this happens; do NOT revert back to your other person (the one who doesn't want to be professional, the sensitive about their work kind of person, etc.).

Choose in this moment to be mature and wise in how you handle "the complainer," "the never satisfied", and in my personal opinion the worst kind…"the micromanager".  All these types of customer/clients can be enough to make you want to scream, holla, curse, and quit the business (on your worse days), but remember that no matter what they do and say, you're obligated to stay professional, and you have the character, the wisdom, and the intelligence to deal with any client in a kind and respectful manner; even if you must put your fake smile on to do it.

People judge entrepreneurs and the small business very harshly. They will expect more from you than they do from big and established corporations. Your product/service quality will be the same if not better than the big-name stores and companies, but they will still try to make it seem like you and your business has such a lower standard or quality. Don't take the accusations and insinuations personal because it is a common misconception that every entrepreneur endures at some point. Just be intentional with the way you do business and try to be understanding enough to know that every customer/client is an opportunity to prove that misconception to be false.

Most consumers don't comprehend that both the small and large companies are ordering products and supplies from the same manufacturers and suppliers (especially in retail). The difference is that the big corporations exist strictly for profit and even though they're getting a lower price on the products they will still overly markup the product to increase their profit margin.

The small business will buy that same product but at a much higher cost and slightly mark it up to make a small profit, just to provide for their families. They do this because they know that the average consumer is reluctant to buy expensive items from the local business.

Every business, both small and big have flaws and make errors. The ironic part is that sometimes it's the smaller company with the most to lose, they will actually go the extra mile to make it right while meanwhile you can't even get a customer service representative on the phone from the big companies to take your complaint or fix your problem quickly and efficiently.

Oftentimes your everyday consumer doesn't always know and understand the disadvantages you face or have to deal with as a small business owner. Don't be discouraged by the customer who isn't satisfied with your efforts at all. You can't make everyone happy all the time (even in business), but your only obligation is to try to make any wrongs, right for your customer/client. If you have done that and they still take their business elsewhere or talk badly about you and your business; then be mature enough to let it go with a smile, knowing that all business just isn't good business.

# 10
## *Boss Up*

There's not enough time or paper to give you every success nugget for entrepreneurship, but through this book I have been able to give you the major keys to success that life, experiences, and God's wisdom and revelations have shown me. The truth is, that God has ordained you to be wealthy. He wants you to be a person of influence; emotionally, financially, spiritually, and relationally.

Deuteronomy 8:18 is ALL the confirmation any of us need to truly understand that God's plan and written will for our lives is to be prosperous. The scripture reads: *"But thou shalt **remember** the Lord thy **God**: for it is HE that **giveth** thee **power** to **get wealth**, that **HE** may **establish HIS covenant** which HE sware unto thy fathers, as it is this day."*

Entrepreneurship is "power" to "get wealth". This scripture alone reveals many things to us. It firstly, lets us know that when God is your source and the inspiration behind your ambitions, He shows you exactly how to achieve that mission. By utilizing the natural gifts, talents, and wisdom you possess, you are already in the greatest position to move forward into your wealth.

Creativity, knowledge, and ability are all crucial components to entrepreneurship. These areas reveal what product or service you can use as an avenue to entrepreneurship. However, after you begin to actively build your business, you often observe and discover other areas where the business can expand in because of your experience, talent, and/or knowledge base.

I remember being a two-time divorced, single mother of three young children. I didn't want to leave my home to work a nine to five job, because I felt that my children needed me to be there for them. I wanted to ensure that they would grow and develop the way God wanted them to. I had a desire to guide them, spend time with them, and allow them to feel the presence and love of at least one of their parents.

Although I had that desire, I wasn't blind nor naïve to the fact that the bills would not pay themselves, nor that food and clothing would magically manifest.

I had to be able to bring finances into our home. I prayed to God, and before I could really seek an answer, God began to show me Deuteronomy 8:18. I knew in the revelation of this scripture that God was calling me to do something that I personally, had never seen anyone around me do, which was work for myself. I promise you all that I had no idea what that meant at that time. I didn't even look at it as being an entrepreneur (that verbiage was foreign to me).

I was just trying to find a way to support myself and my three children without any help. God connected me with an entrepreneur from my church who had his own construction company. My Pastor and "adopted father" referred me to him because he needed some office work done and he knew that I had clerical skills and had gone to college for Business Administration. The gentleman not only hired me to do a few jobs for him, but it became my steady, work from home source of income. God came through like he always does.

My new boss and I became close like brother and sister. He saw the struggles I was having, and he did more than just be a boss he became a brother. He bought me a computer to do work not just for him, but to expand my capabilities to make money by getting other clients. He also bought me a car so that I could move around with my kids. I worked for him for ten years and when I re-located to a different city to start my new life; he took me to his accountant who organized and filed my legal paperwork to establish my very first business, and he paid for it all. I am forever grateful for the seeds that have been sown into my life when I was a young entrepreneur by more experienced entrepreneurs, because it has formed the very foundation that I have built upon now as I become more successful by the day.

It's not just your spiritual gifts that make room for you, but your natural ones will too. He was impressed with my work and my work ethic. I was a young woman with three small children, but I never missed a deadline. There was never coffee, milk, or cheetoh stains on the paperwork. He allowed me to stay home and work to be with my children because he understood my desire to be home with them to teach and raise them.

I continually teach my business mentee's that entrepreneurship is not just based on your skills, talents, and products. It's also based upon "impartation". Knowledge alone does not make you a successful entrepreneur.

According to the Merriam-Webster's online dictionary the word impart means: 1) to give, convey, or grant from or as if from a store 2) to communicate the knowledge of. Which in laymen's terms just means that the spirit of entrepreneurship can be transferred from one "Boss" to another.

After working with my brother and listening to his dreams and long-term goals for business and expansion, I was inspired. I believe that God was watering my mindset, my spirit, and my creative ability even in those moments. I received an impartation of entrepreneurship because I worked with one.

I never thought that I'd be where I am today. I just thought that I was great at office work. The most I was hoping for, was to be an Executive Assistant one day, after my children had gotten older and climbed up the company ladder to

Manager at best. However, God had a different plan for me and my life, just like he has for yours.

Some people are happy working a nine to five job that they love or working in the career field they went to college to be prepared for. There is absolutely nothing wrong with that, but some of you, will do that for a season: un-fulfilled until the day that God calls you off your jobs and careers to take the biggest faith leap of all into entrepreneurship. Everyone worries about the right timing but trust me; when it's time for you to leap you will know it, feel it, and believe it with everything in you; despite the small voice of doubt within you.

God has NOT given us the spirit of "fear" but of "love", "power", and a "sound mind". No matter what insecurities or doubts you or others may have placed within your heart and spirit. I challenge and urge you to not allow anything nor anyone to stop the progression of success that's hitting your life right now. If you're already taking the leap into entrepreneurship don't quit, don't be discouraged, and don't focus on the negative in any aspect. Friends will start acting funny, relationships may become distant or even crash. Family may turn into haters, no matter what oppositions you are faced with…KEEP MOVING! The race is not given to the swift, nor is the battle given to the strong, but it is given to the ONE that endures until the end.

This is the time, TODAY…RIGHT NOW, to remove all doubt and fear. It's time to make your choice to simply, "BOSS UP". It's a new day, a new you, and a new level of success. Go for it with everything you've got, knowing that this was the life God had pre-destined for your life from your mother's womb.

If you think like an entrepreneur; I promise you that eventually you will build yourself and your brand to a place where you can now live like a "Boss". Your place of success is the place where you will be able to change the dynamic of your family, community, and the mindset of those around you. Many entrepreneurs have dreams of helping others and becoming a source of resource and education to build more community and familial wealth. This should be a goal for all entrepreneurs. The hard work and discipline you must partake in at the beginning stages of your entrepreneurial journey is what will make the end goal possible.

I also have the desire to be a change agent. I desire to change my personal station within my community and the communities I grew up in. Becoming successful, gains the attention of others. It's your place of success that causes people to stop and listen to the wisdom and instructions that come from your experiences, knowledge, and successful endeavors.

Don't take it personal when people see your beginning stages and don't recognize the mogul, you're on your way to becoming someone truly great! Everyone cannot recognize treasure when it's still covered in the coal, so don't take the opinions of others personal. Instead keep working and building yourself and your business.

Become a daily example to anyone who encounters you that entrepreneurship is the key to many of life's imbalances and struggles. Believe in yourself and always know that God has ordained you to prosper regardless of what anyone else believes or thinks.

# About the Author

Jacqueline "Jackie" Johnson is a mother, entrepreneur, spiritual leader, mentor, and author. She is a woman who although she's a "Boss" in her own rights; choses to be the backbone for so many other entrepreneurs, ministries, leaders, youth and women through the work she does to undergird and mentor others within so many different areas of life.

She is a woman of great wisdom, knowledge, compassion, and spiritual insight. Her vast and diverse life experiences have made her a powerful voice of advocacy within communities allover the nation as she mentors, writes, and publishes books, facilitates multiple podcasts (*Wife Talks, Sister Conversations in Black, Uncut & Unfiltered with Jackie & Latoria, & Boss My Life*), and even teaches on diverse platforms on the topics of love, marriage, parenting, divorce, business, and spirituality. Her transparency, honesty, and relativity, as well as her boldness allows her to deal with these topics on a level that most cannot. She is truly a gem in the business, spiritual, and familial realms, as she seeks to embody balance within her own personal life in addition to teaching others to strive for the same quality of life.

This woman of God is encouraged, held to accountability, and continuously supported by her Spiritual Mother and leader; Apostle/Dr. Dorvetta Price of True Prophetic Utterance Ministries located in Indianapolis, IN. She fellowships and is locally a part of Hill City Church Los Angeles under the leadership of Pastors Deitrick & Dominque Haddon.

# FOLLOW JACKIE JOHNSON

 INSTAGRAM: @thebossmentorj

 TWITTER: @bossqueenjackie

WEBSITEs: www.thebossmentor.org, www.mysistahandme.com, www.p31wivesclub.com

## For Booking Contact our Office:

(323) 405-1218 or email: iamapostlej@gmail.com

## OTHER BOOKS FROM THIS AUTHOR

### Boss Pearls

30 Day Devotional & Journal for Entrepreneurs: $21.00
AVAILABLE: www.thebossmentor.org and
www.amazon.com

### Boss Chronicles

Business book for entrepreneurs: $14.99
AVAILABLE: www.thebossmentor.org and
www.amazon.com

## The Boss Journal

Boss Chronicles Workbook: $16.99
AVAILABLE: www.thebossmentor.org and www.amazon.com

## Matters of the Heart

A book on healing God's way: $14.99
AVAILABLE: www.thebossmentor.org and www.amazon.com

## Back to the Basics
*A great book for discipleship & Leadership training*:
$14.99

AVAILABLE: www.thebossmentor.org and www.amazon.com

## The Secret Diary Vol.1
**"Daddy's Baby" 2nd Edition**: $14.99

AVAILABLE: www.thebossmentor.org and www.amazon.com

## I Came While You Were Sleeping
$14.99

AVAILABLE: www.p31wivesclub.com,
www.thebossmentor.org and www.amazon.com

## Relationship Status
$14.99

AVAILABLE: www.thebossmentor.org,
www.mysistahandme.com/shop
and www.amazon.com

www.ingramcontent.com/pod-product-compliance
Lightning Source LLC
Chambersburg PA
CBHW052334220526
45472CB00001B/422